FOCUS ON GEOGRAPHY

Focus on
Brazil

Natalie Hyde

A Crabtree Forest Book

Crabtree Publishing
crabtreebooks.com

Author: Natalie Hyde

Series research and development:
Janine Deschenes

Editorial director: Kathy Middleton

Editor: Janine Deschenes

Proofreader: Melissa Boyce

Design: Tammy McGarr

IMAGE CREDITS

iStock: Caíque de Abreu, p 40 (bottom);

Shutterstock: F de Jesus, cover (top right); David Fadul, p 11 (top); Renan Martelli da Rosa, p 12 (top); A.PAES, p 12 (bottom), p 22 (top); Tarcisio Schnaider, p 13 (top); renatopmeireles, p 13 (bottom); Joa Souza, p 14 (top), p 42; Antonio Salaverry, p 14 (middle); Alessandro Zappalorto, p 14 (bottom); Christyam de Lima, p 15 (bottom); CYSUN, p 17 (top); Nelson Antoine, p 17 (middle); FLAVIO LEAO, p 19 (top); ViniciusReisBR, p 20 (top); Vitoriano Junior, p 21 (top); Nowaczyk, p 21 (bottom); T photography, p 22 (bottom); Erich Sacco, p 23 (top); Parilov, p 23 (bottom); Alf Ribeiro, p 24, p 30 (bottom); Nido Huebl, p 25 (top right); Kostas Koutsaftikis, p 26 (top left); Midary, p 26 (bottom left); cabuscaa, p 27 (bottom); Wandering views, p 28 (top); BW Press, p 28 (bottom); Vanessa Volk, p 29 (middle right); Sandra Moraes, p 31 (top); Laszlo Mates, p 32 (top); Shawn Eastman Photography, p 33 (top); R.M. Nunesp 33 (bottom); Chaquito, p 34 (top); Erica Catarina Pontes, p 34 (bottom); Maarten Zeehandelaar, p 35 (top); guentermanau, p 38 (bottom); Dado Photos, p 44; eisegraf.ch p 45 (bottom);

Wikimedia Commons: Robson Esteves Czaban, p 9 (top); Carlos Julião, p 18 (bottom); AFP/SCANPIX, p 26 (top right); Nayeryouakim, p 33 (bottom); Mateus Pereira Secom, p 37 (bottom left); Almanaque Lusofonista, p 37 (bottom right); Carl de Souza/AFP, p 42; INPE, p 42;

Crabtree Publishing

crabtreebooks.com   800-387-7650
Copyright © 2024 Crabtree Publishing

Hardcover   978-1-0398-1521-6
Paperback   978-1-0398-1547-6
Ebook (pdf)   978-1-0398-1599-5
Epub   978-1-0398-1573-5

Published in Canada
Crabtree Publishing
616 Welland Avenue
St. Catharines, Ontario
L2M 5V6

Published in the United States
Crabtree Publishing
347 Fifth Avenue
Suite 1402-145
New York, New York, 10016

Library and Archives Canada Cataloguing in Publication
Available at Library and Archives Canada

Library of Congress Cataloging-in-Publication Data
Available at the Library of Congress

Printed in the U.S.A./072023/CG20230214

Contents

Introduction

There are 12 to 24 Brazil nuts wedged inside each husk.

The Amazon rain forest's land and water ecosystems provide food and water to an estimated 34 million people.

Harvesting the Rain Forest

On a March morning, villagers walk in single file down a trail in the Amazon rain forest of Brazil. They will head deep into the forest to harvest Brazil nuts. Unlike many crops grown on farms or **plantations**, Brazil nuts are harvested from large trees in the wild. Brazil nut trees can grow up to 197 feet (60 m) tall and live for hundreds of years. Many live to 1,000 years old! From December to March, which is summer in the **Southern Hemisphere**, many villagers walk for hours each day to begin their work.

Nut harvesters look for fruits that have fallen into the thick rainforest **undergrowth**. At the same time, they must watch carefully for snakes and poisonous insects that also live there. The nuts are in hard husks, like coconuts. When the husks fall from the tall trees, they can cause severe injuries or even death if they hit the harvesters.

Villagers use machetes to slice open the husks and shake the nuts into their bags. Each metal pail, called a *latas*, filled with Brazil nuts earns them about 45 to 50 Brazilian reais (about 8 or 9 U.S. dollars). At the end of the day, harvesters begin the long walk home with heavy sacks of Brazil nuts over their shoulders. Tomorrow, they will start the long trek all over again.

The equator passes through Brazil. This means 10 percent of the country is in the Northern Hemisphere. The remaining 90 percent lies in the Southern Hemisphere.

Get to Know Brazil

The country of Brazil is officially called the Federative Republic of Brazil. Measuring 2,700 miles (4,350 km) from north to south, it is the largest country in South America and makes up half of the continent's land mass. Brazil shares land borders with every other country in South America except for Chile and Ecuador. It has a population of about 214 million people and its capital city is Brasília.

AT A GLANCE

- **OFFICIAL NAME:** Federative Republic of Brazil

- **NATIONAL CAPITAL:** Brasília

- **POPULATION:** 214,891,000

- **OFFICIAL LANGUAGE:** Portuguese

- **LAND AREA:** 3,282,922 square miles (8,502,728 sq. km)

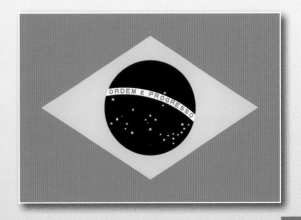

From North to South

Brazil is divided into five major regions. They are the North, Northeast, Central-West, Southeast, and South. These regions are then divided into a total of 26 states. Each region has its own unique landforms and natural resources.

The North consists mostly of rain forest and some highlands. The rain forest is part of the Amazon River basin and represents half of the world's remaining rain forests. The Amazon rain forest is home to one-third of all species of animals in the world. The North region does not have many large settlements or **industries**.

The Federal District is a special, self-governing region separate from Brazil's states.

The Northeast is the driest and hottest area of the country. About 30 percent of the people in Brazil live in this region. There is some agriculture here, but many people who live in this region are still looking for employment.

The Central-West region contains the Federal District with the capital city, Brasília. This region has forested valleys, **semi-arid** highlands and large wetlands. The beauty of the landscape makes it popular for **ecotourism**.

The Southeast is the second-smallest region, but it has the most industrial and agricultural production. It is an important center for mining as well as tourism. One of the best-known cities, Rio de Janeiro, or Rio, is in this region. Rio is famous for its Carnival celebration (see page 34). The Southeast is also home to São Paulo, a large industrial center.

The South region is the smallest in Brazil. However, its mild **climate** makes it a leader in agriculture in the country. It is also the largest coal-producing region. Many cities in the South region are strong in manufacturing, including shoes and cars.

Iguaçu National Park, in the South region, has one of the world's largest waterfalls. It is also home to many endangered animals, including the giant otter and giant anteater.

Brazil is home to seven natural **UNESCO World Heritage Sites**, including the Pantanal Conservation Area in the Central-West region. One of the world's largest freshwater wetland ecosystems is found there.

The Land

Brazil is the fifth-largest country in the world, covering more than 3 million square miles (8 million sq. km). It has many kinds of landscapes, including low mountains, **plateaus**, grassy plains called savannas, and wetlands. Brazil's landforms can be divided into five main regions: the Amazon basin, the Guiana Highlands, the Pantanal, the Brazilian Highlands, and the Coastal Lowlands.

The Amazon basin is a lowland area that is drained by the Amazon River and its **tributaries**, or the smaller rivers and creeks that flow into it. Most of the basin is covered by the Amazon rain forest. These lowlands include areas right along the river that flood each year. They also include lakes, wetlands, and rolling hills that were formed by **sediment** from the Amazon River.

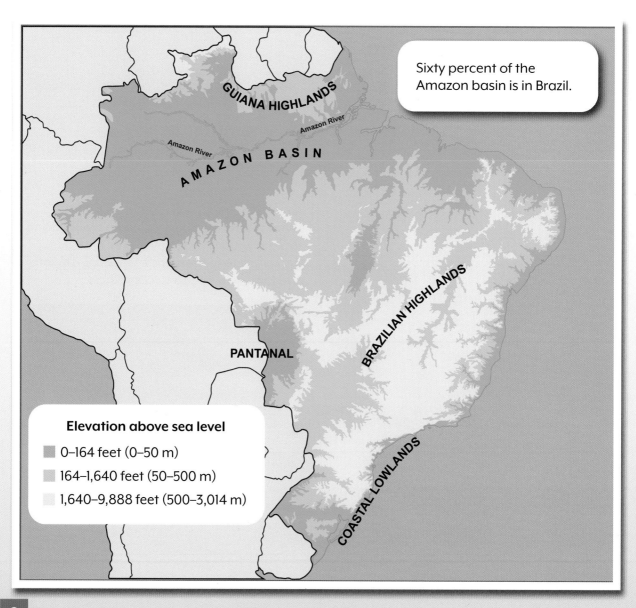

Sixty percent of the Amazon basin is in Brazil.

GUIANA HIGHLANDS

Amazon River

Amazon River

A M A Z O N   B A S I N

BRAZILIAN HIGHLANDS

PANTANAL

COASTAL LOWLANDS

Elevation above sea level

■ 0–164 feet (0–50 m)

■ 164–1,640 feet (50–500 m)

■ 1,640–9,888 feet (500–3,014 m)

Highlands and Lowlands

North of the Amazon basin are the Guiana Highlands. The relatively low mountain ranges there contain the highest land elevations in the country. Southwest of the Amazon basin and hugging Brazil's western border with Bolivia is the Pantanal. This is one of the largest freshwater wetlands in the world, with huge swamps and marshes.

The Brazilian Highlands cover more than half of the country. The highlands include flat-topped hills called plateaus, **ravines**, and rolling hills. They contain valuable minerals such as gold and diamonds. Along the Atlantic coast of Brazil are the Coastal Lowlands. This narrow strip of land is only 125 miles (200 km) at its widest point. It contains **floodplains**, swamps, lagoons, sand dunes, and white-sand beaches.

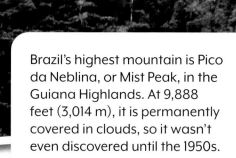

Brazil's highest mountain is Pico da Neblina, or Mist Peak, in the Guiana Highlands. At 9,888 feet (3,014 m), it is permanently covered in clouds, so it wasn't even discovered until the 1950s.

The Pampas are flat grasslands located in the southernmost part of the country. The area is especially important to certain bird species that are not found anywhere else, such as the Pampas meadowlark.

Water Systems

Brazil has around 13 percent of the world's water. Most of it is found in the Amazon River basin. In other parts of the country, such as the Southeast region, there is very little water. Brazil has 2,858 miles (4,600 km) of coastline. Off the coast are many islands, coral reefs, and bays. The coast of Brazil is famous for its beautiful beaches, making it a popular destination for tourists and vacationers.

Stretching around 4,345 miles (6,992 km), the Amazon River is the largest river in the world by **volume** and one of the longest. Just one of the Amazon's tributaries, the Rio Negro, is about 1,400 miles (2,250 km) long and carries more water than the Mississippi River. The Amazon **originates** in the Andes Mountains in Peru and flows eastward to empty into the Atlantic Ocean. It is wide and deep enough to be used for transportation from the ocean into the Amazon rain forest. Large ships can navigate upstream to the city of Manaus, 900 miles (1,450 km) from the coast. Smaller boats can travel 2,300 miles (3,700 km) inland, all the way to Peru.

Although many of the Amazon's tributaries, such as the Urubu River, are also large and deep, ships cannot travel far up them because of waterfalls and rapids.

Rio de Janeiro, on the southeast coast, is one of the most popular tourist cities in South America.

Brazil is one of the top 10 countries in the world in the use of irrigation for livestock and growing crops.

Brazil also has other important river systems. The Paraguay-Paraná-Plata is the second-biggest river system. It drains the South and Southeast regions. There are many **hydroelectric** power plants along the tributaries of this river system. Other water systems are used to channel water for **irrigation**. In the Southeast region, this is mainly to flood **rice paddies**.

Closer Look

Bahia Mangroves

The Bahia mangroves in northeastern Brazil are tidal areas where groups of trees and shrubs grow. The ecosystem is threatened by rising water levels and temperatures because of **climate change**. These changes threaten marine animals, such as crabs, which puts the ecosystem's entire food chain at risk. All mangroves in Brazil are legally designated as "permanent protection zones." They absorb a large amount of **carbon dioxide**, making them very important in facing climate change. They are also biodiverse areas, home to many plant and animal species.

The Bahia mangroves are home to five endangered species of sea turtles: loggerhead, green (above), leatherback, hawksbill, and olive.

Mangroves cover 5,401 square miles (13,989 sq. km) along Brazil's coast. This is an area larger than the island of Hawaii!

Natural Resources

Brazil has a wealth of natural resources. It is a mining leader in many kinds of minerals. It benefits from the water of the Amazon River and the power it creates. Brazil is also one of the top oil producers in the world.

There are more than 3,000 mines in Brazil. Most are located in the state of Minas Gerais in the Southeast region. Metals such as iron, aluminum, copper, tin, and gold make up more than 80 percent of the minerals mined. Brazil is the second-largest iron **ore exporter** in the world. The country is also a source of precious gemstones such as amethysts, aquamarines, and diamonds.

Timber is another important natural resource for Brazil. Sixty percent of the country is covered in forests. Most timber is harvested in the South and Southeast regions, from plantations of eucalyptus and pine trees. Most of this timber is used for paper products. However, hardwood trees found in the Amazon basin, such as mahogany trees, are illegally logged.

Brazil is the largest oil producer in South America. Almost all oil wells are located off the coast, near the city of Rio de Janeiro. Brazil is now **self-sufficient** in oil. It produces 3 million and uses 2.5 million barrels of oil per day. Brazil still imports some oil, however, because its oil refineries are not able to process enough crude oil to meet the country's needs.

More than 180,000 people are employed in Brazil's mining industry.

Brazil exported 357.7 million tons (324.5 metric tons) of iron ore in 2021.

Some reports say that 80 to 90 percent of logging in the Amazon rain forest is illegal. Logging companies may cut protected trees, fell more trees than allowed, and steal land from protected areas and **Indigenous** peoples.

Guanabara Bay, off of Rio de Janeiro, is home to much offshore oil exploration. It is also the site of three major oil spills, causing serious damage to plant and animal life there.

Major Settlements

São Paulo

São Paulo is located on a plateau of the Brazilian Highlands in the Southeast region. The valleys below the city are **fertile** farmland, largely used for coffee plantations, and the rivers are a route into the interior. The city was important to the state of Minas Gerais during the gold rush in the 1600s, when it became a gateway for **prospectors**. This mineral wealth, and a demand for coffee, transformed it from a poor village to one of the richest cities in Brazil.

Rio de Janeiro

Portuguese explorers first landed in Guanabara Bay in January 1502. They named the spot Rio de Janeiro—January River. It is surrounded by plains of the western shore of Guanabara Bay. This land was used for sugarcane plantations and the profits helped the city grow. Rio's location along the coast of the Atlantic means it is well-known for beautiful beaches.

Today, São Paulo is a center for automobile manufacturing, with major manufacturing plants there owned by companies such as Toyota and Mercedes-Benz.

Rio de Janeiro was an important center in the Portuguese **empire**. The Portuguese royal family moved there in 1808 and lived in the *Paço Imperial*, or Imperial Palace, below.

Manaus (see opposite page) is a launching spot for tourism as visitors explore the Amazon River basin.

ATLANTIC OCEAN

Manaus

BRAZIL

PACIFIC OCEAN

Belo Horizonte

Rio de Janeiro

São Paulo

ATLANTIC OCEAN

Manaus

Manaus lies along the north bank of the Rio Negro tributary, just above where it joins the Amazon River. Rubber from rubber trees in the area brought wealth to the city, making it the richest city in South America in the late 1800s. Today, Manaus is a major **inland port** used by ships from the Atlantic. It is also a trade center of the Amazon basin, receiving fish from fish farms, cattle from savannas up the Branco River tributary, and Brazil nuts.

Belo Horizonte

The capital city of the state of Minas Gerais, Belo Horizonte is the sixth-largest city in Brazil. It is built on several hills and is completely surrounded by mountains. Much of its wealth comes from the rich agricultural and mining land around it. Gold, manganese, and gemstones mined in the region are processed in the city.

Established in 1897, Belo Horizonte is now home to around 2.7 million people.

Climate and Weather

Brazil has a mostly humid tropical and subtropical climate. A tropical climate means it is warm all year round, with an average temperature of 64 degrees Fahrenheit (18 °C) in the coolest month. Subtropical zones are usually located to the north and south of tropical zones. They can experience slightly cooler temperatures.

One exception to the tropical and subtropical climate is an area in the northeast corner of Brazil, where the climate is drier. This region receives just 15 to 30 inches (38 to 76 cm) of precipitation a year. It can sometimes suffer from **droughts**—but at other times can have severe storms and floods.

Most of Brazil receives 40 to 70 inches (101 to 178 cm) of rain per year. That is similar to Vancouver or New York City. The central parts of the Brazilian Highlands can have **torrential** downpours in the summer months, from November to April. In the winter months, from May to October, the highlands are often dry. Frost can even occur in winter there.

Constant Conditions

The tropical climate of the Amazon basin means that the temperature does not change much throughout the year. There is a "dry" and a "wet" season, but most of the time there isn't much difference between the two. The dry season may have less rainfall, but it still rains consistently.

The varied weather conditions—from drought to flooding—can make life difficult for people living in the Northeast. It is a significant reason that many migrate out of the region.

Snow can fall in the high plains of the South region of Brazil, but elsewhere it is rare.

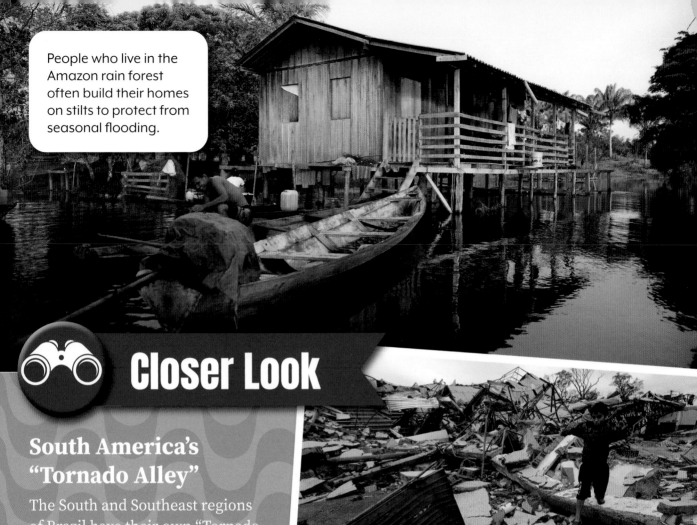

People who live in the Amazon rain forest often build their homes on stilts to protect from seasonal flooding.

Closer Look

South America's "Tornado Alley"

The South and Southeast regions of Brazil have their own "Tornado Alley." Along with regions in the surrounding countries of Argentina, Paraguay, and Uruguay, this area has one of the highest frequencies of tornadoes in the world—though it does not come close to the high frequency of tornadoes in the United States. The weather patterns in this area of Brazil create the perfect tornado conditions. Across the flat Pampas plains, cold air coming up from Antarctica collides with warm air from northern Brazil. These collisions produce thunderstorms, in which tornadoes can form. Cities such as Rio de Janeiro have a siren alert system to warn of dangerous weather.

Tornadoes in 2015 and 2020 in Santa Catarina, a state in Brazil's South region, have left hundreds of people without homes.

Researchers are finding that severe storms such as tornadoes are on the increase due to **global warming**.

Becoming Brazil

It is estimated that there were once around 2,000 different Indigenous tribes and nations in what is now Brazil, each with its own culture and customs.

Archaeological sites show that parts of Brazil may have been **inhabited** since 9000 B.C.E. Indigenous peoples living in the Amazon lowlands were farmers, fishers, and hunters. Groups on the plains and in the highlands were hunter-gatherers. Many were semi-**nomadic** and moved with the seasons. Between 2 and 6 million Indigenous peoples lived in Brazil at the time of European contact in the 1500s.

Portuguese explorers were looking for a route to India from Portugal. The Tupian-speaking people who lived along the coast were the first to encounter the Portuguese as they landed on the Brazilian coast. The wealth of natural resources and the number of safe ports for ships led to the explorers claiming the land now known as Brazil for Portugal. As more Europeans arrived, they brought diseases with them. These diseases caused the deaths of millions of Indigenous peoples. Those that survived often suffered brutal treatment under the Portuguese.

The Portuguese **enslaved** Indigenous peoples and exploited their labor to increase their wealth.

Brazil gained independence from Portugal on September 7, 1822, when Portuguese prince Dom Pedro declared the country's independence and was crowned emperor. The date is celebrated today as a national holiday.

Riches at a Cost

Europeans began to move from coastal areas into the interior. **Missionaries** were spreading Christianity, while cattlemen were looking for more **pastureland**. Some settlers, called *bandeirantes*, moved westward. They wanted to capture Indigenous people and enslave them. In doing so, the *bandeirantes* strengthened Portugal's power over the territory. They searched for gold and precious stones at the same time.

The gold rush in 1690 started when *bandeirantes* discovered a large amount of gold in the mountains of Minas Gerais. Brazil soon supplied half the global demand for gold. More than 400,000 Portuguese came to the region. Portugal also sent more than 500,000 enslaved people from Africa to work in the mines. Brazil's economy and society revolved around mining and agriculture, mainly sugar. The wealth from these industries mostly came from the work of enslaved people. Brazil was the last country in South America to abolish slavery in 1888.

Slavery lasted more than 300 years in Brazil. It is estimated that more than 4 million enslaved Africans were sent there. Other estimates are even higher. It was their labor that built the Brazilian economy.

CABIN

Railroads are mostly used to transport **freight** or move people within urban areas.

Early Transportation

The earliest transportation routes into the interior of Brazil were natural waterways, mainly the Amazon River system. It is still the easiest way to access some of the country's **remote** areas. Waterways are used mainly to transport agricultural and mineral products. Brazil's National Transport Confederation, however, identifies water transportation as an area with a lot of potential. Just 30 percent of Brazil's existing water network is used today.

The first railroad in Brazil was built in 1835. Railroads were used to connect mineral-producing regions to ocean ports. The railroad routes were limited because of the dense Amazon rain forest and many rivers. This is why the railroads did not lead to the settlement of the interior. The other problem was that different companies created railroad lines with different-sized tracks. This made it difficult to link rail lines across the country. The rail system is almost entirely in the eastern half of the country.

Brazil's many waterways could provide a much wider transportation network, through which goods and people could travel inland and to and from major ports.

Because of their affordability, buses are the leading means of transportation in Brazil. Brazilian bus companies have invested in more comfortable buses with air conditioning and reclining chairs.

In 1956, former president of Brazil Juscelino Kubitschek began to build a new capital city for the country. Brasília was built in an **unpopulated** area that was in a central location—but getting there was difficult. So the government began a large program to develop a road system to get to and from the new capital. By the 1990s, Brazil's road system was the third-longest in the new world. Today, the system of paved highways connects all major cities in Brazil.

Brazil has the second-largest number of airports in the world. That is because air travel is the fastest way to access Brazil's many remote areas. In turn, people living in these remote regions depend on air transport for supplies. More than 800,000 jobs in Brazil support the air transport industry.

Dugout canoes, carved from tree trunks, were among the first boats made and used by humans. These canoes are still made and used in southern and southeastern Brazil for fishing.

Mining Roots

Mining in Brazil began with gold being found above ground, in rivers and streams. When these resources were gone, companies began **extracting** gold from underground. In the 1800s, other minerals such as coal, oil, and iron were discovered and mined.

Brazil was the first country in the West to produce diamonds. Like gold, the first diamonds were found in the soil in riverbeds in the 1700s. For 100 years after that, Brazil was the world leader in producing diamonds. Mining companies today face the challenge of balancing mining activities with protecting the sensitive ecosystems of the river systems. Another problem is regulating diamond mining around Indigenous communities to protect their land and lifestyles.

Iron ore

Mining activities are linked to **deforestation** and biodiversity loss in the Amazon rain forest, as well as the contamination of Brazil's rivers with **toxic** chemicals.

Hydroelectric power plants provide more than 60 percent of Brazil's energy needs.

Energy Production

The first hydro plant in Brazil came into operation in 1883. It was built on the river Ribeirão do Inferno to power a **textile** mill. Dams were built on other rivers to produce hydroelectric power for homes and appliances. Today, Brazil has the largest hydroelectric power production in South America. There are more than 200 power stations. Nuclear power started with the Angra 1 power plant in Rio de Janeiro in 1982. Today, Brazil has two nuclear reactors that generate about 3 percent of its electricity. A third plant is under construction.

Coal mining is a large part of Brazil's economy. While it helps the economy, environmental damage, especially in the South region, is a concern.

Brazil has huge oil reserves. There are many oil and natural gas fields off the coast. These deposits sit along the continental shelf, or the shallow edge of a continent that sits under the sea. Brazil is now the largest oil producer in South America. While most of the world is pulling back on oil use and production, Brazil is planning to expand its oil production in the coming years.

Subsistence farming is prominent in some areas of Brazil. This means farmers grow just enough food to support themselves and their families.

Around 40,000 Brazilians work in the leather-manufacturing industry.

Growing and Building

Agriculture in Brazil began with Indigenous peoples, who farmed crops such as peanuts, tobacco, **cassavas**, and maize, or corn. When the Portuguese arrived, they were interested in the brazilwood trees for lumber and the valuable red dye that could be made from it. This is how Brazil got its name and is one reason that the Portuguese wanted control of the country.

Sugarcane plantations in Brazil began with the arrival of the Portuguese 500 years ago. At that time, sugarcane and gold had almost the same value. About 100 years later, Brazil was the biggest sugar producer in the world. It often still takes the top spot of global sugar producers. Today, sugarcane can also be used to produce ethanol. Ethanol is a liquid used to make plastics, cosmetics, polishes, and **biofuel**. It is also used in alcoholic drinks and as a disinfectant.

A large part of Brazil's economy is manufacturing. The textile industry began in 1814, using local supplies of cotton. This expanded into leather footwear, using hides left over from meat processing. Brazil is also a major world supplier of automobiles. Brazilian workers produce more than 2 million vehicles per year. Other factories produce soap, medicine, chemicals, paints, steel, and paper.

Tourism

Tourism is a growing industry in Brazil. Many tourists head to Rio de Janeiro with its festivals, good hotels and restaurants, and beautiful beaches. Ecotourism is tourism focused on natural environments and it supports the conservation of habitats and animals. The Amazon basin is a popular destination for ecotourism. Brazil's 4,600-mile (7,400 km) Atlantic coast is lined with sandy beaches, drawing visitors from around the world.

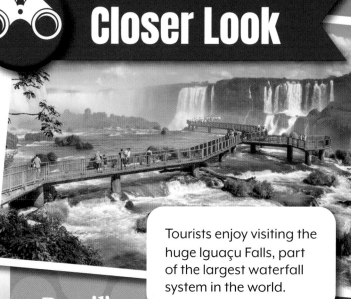

Tourists enjoy visiting the huge Iguaçu Falls, part of the largest waterfall system in the world.

Brazil's National Parks

There are 70 national parks in Brazil. The first parks were created in the 1930s. The goal of the parks is to preserve ecosystems and to support scientific research, education, and ecotourism. Today, 21 national parks protect different areas of the Amazon rain forest in Brazil. They help protect biodiversity and natural resources in the area. The Tumucumaque National Park, for example, is part of the largest protected tropical rain forest in the world. The Anavilhanas National Park is a habitat for many protected species, such as the Amazon river dolphin.

Rio's Copacabana beach has been named one of the top 10 beaches in the world.

The Amazon river dolphin is also known as the pink river dolphin because of its distinctive color. It is found in freshwater rivers in South America.

Life Today

Pelé was born in the city of Três Corações, in Minas Gerais. He is considered a national hero.

Pélé

Sports and Recreation

Brazilians are huge sports fans. Football, or soccer, is the nation's most popular sport. It is played by young and old, professional and **amateur**. The world-famous football player Pelé was from Brazil. International football matches held in the major cities draw huge crowds.

Some say that Brazilians are great football players because, as children, they play a game called *futsal*. There are not too many full-sized football fields in Brazil because of the cost and space needed on flat land. *Futsal*, however, is played indoors on a small court. This gives more people access to the skills that make them good football players. Brazil has qualified for every FIFA World Cup tournament since it began in 1930, and has won the title five times.

It's common to find Brazilian children playing football in the streets of their neighborhoods.

Capoeira is the national sport of Brazil. It is a martial art that combines elements of dance, acrobatics, and music. It was originally created by enslaved Africans in Brazil.

Peteca is a game that has its origins in Indigenous groups. It is like a cross between badminton and volleyball. It uses a feathered shuttlecock or "birdie" like badminton, but is hit over a high net with the hand, like volleyball. Beach volleyball is another popular sport. The miles of sandy beaches in Brazil make the sport easily accessible. Communities put up beach volleyball nets so they dot the shoreline all along the coast. Beaches are also popular for swimming, surfing, and relaxing.

Brazil is also the site of a jungle marathon called the "World's Toughest Endurance Race." It is an extreme footrace that takes place in the Amazon rain forest in the Tapajos National Forest. The course includes swamps, river crossings, steep climbs and descents, and village trails in hot, humid weather.

FEBARC is Brazil's Federation of Model Auto Racing. It holds the national championship races at the Beeight track in the city of Cianorte in southern Brazil.

Industry Today

A serious problem Brazil faces today is illegal mining. Since 2010, illegal mining inside Indigenous territories and conservation areas has increased by 400 percent. The increase in global gold prices has led to even more demand, resulting in more illegal mining.

There is a higher chance of finding gold in undisturbed soil. That is why illegal miners target regions that are protected and unused. However, these areas also have the most fragile ecosystems, with plant and animal species that are not found anywhere else. Law enforcement is not as strong and consistent as it could be, so illegal miners are willing to take the risk of getting caught. Illegal mining, unfortunately, also creates jobs. In areas where poverty and unemployment are high, people may join illegal mining activities to make money to survive.

Mining is illegal on Indigenous lands. In 2022, Indigenous peoples protested to protect their territories when mining companies and the Brazilian government eyed them as future mining sites.

Millions of Indigenous peoples depend on the Amazon rain forest for survival. With its destruction, it is increasingly difficult for them to maintain their ways of life.

Although Brazil has a long coastline, its fishing industry is smaller than those in countries such as Argentina or Mexico. The coastal waters are warmed by the Brazil current, and this supports fewer fish than colder water. Most of the fishing industry is fish farming, called aquaculture. Freshwater fish, shrimp, shellfish, and frogs are some of the species farmed in rivers and tributaries. Tilapia, a fast-growing fish, is one of the most popular fish for aquaculture.

With the diversity of plants in the Amazon rain forest, herbal medicines are a growing industry in Brazil. The Indigenous peoples of the Amazon have a long history of using herbal medicines. The Matsés people of Brazil and Peru, for example, created a 500-page encyclopedia of their traditional medicine. Written in their native language, it was compiled by five **shamans** and details every plant used by the Matsés to cure all kinds of ailments.

Indigenous peoples use acai berries, collected in the Amazon rain forest, to reduce swelling and boost the immune system.

Almost 90 percent of Brazil's aquaculture is focused on farming freshwater fish, especially tilapia.

The Brazil current is a warm body of water that moves south along the southern Brazilian coast.

Deforestation is a huge problem caused by Brazil's agriculture industry. Large areas of forest, including the Amazon rain forest, have been cleared to make room to grow crops such as soybeans.

Soybeans

Changing Agriculture

Brazil is in the fortunate position of being almost self-sufficient in basic food needs. This means it produces enough food for its own markets as well as having enough to export to other countries. Having this kind of **food security** is a goal of many countries around the world.

Most of Brazil's agricultural land is in the South, Southeast, and Central-West regions. The Northeast region is too dry and the Amazon basin is too wet for most crops. Brazil has cleared more land for agriculture since **World War II** than most other Latin American countries. There are about 160 million acres (65 million hectares) used for agriculture. That is larger than the entire country of France.

Brazil is the largest global producer of coffee. It produces about a third of the world's coffee.

Though the dry Northeast region of Brazil is not suitable for many crops, it is home to large herds of goats and sheep.

Today, Brazil is a leading exporter of oranges, soybeans, coffee, bananas, and cacao, which is used for making chocolate. Until 1990, coffee beans were the country's most important export. Today, however, Brazil's most important crop is soybeans. Most soybeans are grown on the savannas of the central highlands, called the Cerrado. One-third of the world's oranges are also grown in Brazil. The orange orchards are in an area known as the citrus belt, in the Southeast region.

Brazil also has one of the world's largest livestock populations, with over 230 million **head** of cattle. Grazing lands are mostly in the temperate grasslands in the South and Southeast. Although the North region does not have many people, it has the second-largest herd of cattle in the country. Besides cattle, Brazil is a large poultry exporter and one of the world's top pork producers.

Corn is Brazil's second-largest crop. Because of the country's temperate climate, farmers are able to use the same fields to first grow soybeans, then corn. This **double-cropping** gives Brazil an advantage to export more produce than other countries.

31

A Vibrant Country

Brazil's people have remained remarkably united for such a large country. One common bond is language. Portuguese is spoken by citizens across the entire country, except for some Indigenous peoples, such as those living in remote areas of the Amazon River basin. Brazil's Amazon is home to more **uncontacted** tribes than anywhere else in the world. There are thought to be at least 100 **isolated** groups in the rain forest.

Sixty percent of the Amazon rain forest is in Brazil. Because of this, Brazil is one of the world's most biodiverse countries. It is estimated that there are 4 million different plant and animal species. Incredibly, a new species of plant or animal is discovered in the Amazon about every three days!

There are around 274 different languages spoken by Indigenous peoples in Brazil.

Ilha da Queimada Grande, or Snake Island, in Brazil is home to the critically endangered golden lancehead. The deadly snake is found nowhere else on Earth. It is illegal to visit the island, to protect both people and the snakes.

The Christ the Redeemer statue in Rio de Janeiro has been named one of the New 7 Wonders of the World.

Rio de Janeiro was once not only the capital of Brazil, but also the capital of Portugal. This made it the only European capital city outside of Europe at the time. Rio is also the site for the largest Carnival celebration in the world, with more than 2 million visitors. Brazilian culture is warm and family-centered. Brazilians also have their own way of doing many things. For example, a unique program offers Brazilian prisoners the opportunity to reduce their sentences by reading books. A distinguishing part of Brazilian culture, *jeitinho*, or "a little way," is the practice of accomplishing something by bending the rules.

Brasília, Brazil's modern capital, was built to open up the country's interior. It was a highly modern city at the time it was planned.

Cultures and Traditions

Brazil is a unique blend of cultures and traditions because of its Indigenous groups and European immigrants. Because Portuguese missionaries brought Christianity to South America, many festivals and holidays are Christian, with the majority being of Roman Catholic origin.

One of those Christian festivals is Carnival. It is a celebration before the start of Lent, a time when Christians typically **fast** or give up treats as a way to prepare for Easter. Rio de Janeiro celebrates Carnival in a big way. Over five days, people dance the **samba**, especially at the Copacabana Ball, watch parades with elaborate costumes, and enjoy street parties called *blocos*.

Carnival performers wear elaborate, brightly colored costumes.

Salvador is one of the oldest colonial cities in the Americas. It was used as a major port for the sugar and **slave trade**. Today, it has a thriving Afro-Brazilian culture.

Not all Brazilians are Christian. There is also a regional religion called Candomblé. The word means "dance in honor of the gods." It combines elements from African cultures as well as elements of Catholicism and Indigenous South American beliefs. It was developed by enslaved Africans living in Brazil. It is practiced by at least 2 million Brazilians.

Festa Junina, or June Festival, has European roots. It is a harvest celebration in June, the beginning of winter in the Southern Hemisphere. There are music and costumes, all with the theme of farming and ranching. People dress up as cowboys and cowgirls and dance a *quadrilha*, a square dance with four couples.

The *Banda de Ipanema* is one of the largest Carnival street festivals in Brazil. It is more informal than the Carnival parades and includes music and dancing.

Closer Look

Lunch is a meal to be appreciated in Brazil. People step away from work and enjoy food and conversation with their coworkers.

Feijoada

Wednesday and Saturday are *feijoada* days in Brazil. This national dish is special in the country and often shared with family and friends. It is a stew that includes dark beans, pork meat, and many spices. It is served with rice, onion, vinegar, and tomato salad. It is believed that the dish originated with enslaved people, who created it using leftover food from their enslavers. Some historians, on the other hand, believe the dish was first made by settlers. Despite its disputed origin, *feijoada* is celebrated and enjoyed widely across Brazil.

People in different regions of Brazil modify the ingredients and cooking style of *feijoada*. For example, additional vegetables are often added in the states of Bahia and Sergipe.

The Arts in Brazil

Cave paintings in the Serra da Capivara National Park in the Northeast region are the oldest art form found in Brazil. Some of the images are dated to be 30,000 to 50,000 years old. Many of the caves and rock faces are decorated with paintings of animals and symbols.

Later art was influenced by the Portuguese and other European immigrants. Brazilian folk art usually shows scenes from everyday life. This includes life events, celebrations, fun, and games. Folk art is often made of clay, wood, textiles, or metal. Marajoara pottery originates on Marajó, a small island in the mouth of the Amazon River.

Marajoara pottery

Pots, bowls, and urns were decorated with images of animals such as snakes, turtles, and scorpions.

The cave paintings at Serra da Capivara allow researchers to learn more about the early peoples who lived in the region.

Ecojewelry is made by finding materials in a way that does not harm sensitive ecosystems or use up natural resources. The items are also not created in unsafe environments and workers receive fair wages for the products.

Music has always been a big part of Brazilian celebrations. *Choro* is a music style that has been called the New Orleans jazz of Brazil. It has **instrumental** tunes played with the flute, guitar, or clarinet. The most popular genre in modern Brazilian music is *sertanejo*. It is a mix of country music with cool beats originating from Rio de Janeiro. There are now *sertanejo* clubs and many songs can be heard on Brazilian radio.

Architecture in Brazil reflects the diverse groups and history of the country. Indigenous peoples used, and still use, the materials available to them in their environment. Typically wooden structures are covered with leaves or straw. The Portuguese brought European style and structure to their buildings. The best examples of this are in the city of Salvador, with its multicolored colonial buildings.

Jorge Amado is one of Brazil's best-loved authors. His books reflect the people and customs of his home state, Bahia, and its capital city, Salvador.

Looking to the Future

Shifting Culture

Immigration to Brazil is on the rise. Many people migrate from other countries in South America, such as Venezuela and Bolivia, because they are fleeing natural disasters, looking for jobs, and hoping for a better life. People from the United States, China, and European countries such as Germany and France are also moving to Brazil. Immigrants to Brazil bring their own cultures and traditions.

Kibe

Food is often influenced by the cultures of immigrants. *Kibe* is a snack food in Brazil. It is made from bulgur wheat and chopped meat shaped into **croquettes** that are deep-fried. It arrived with immigrants from Syria and Palestine in the Middle East who were escaping conflict and war in the late 1800s.

São Paulo has a strong Japanese culture. Red-painted archways and shops selling Japanese food and kitchenware can be found throughout the city. Today, São Paulo is home to the world's largest community of Japanese **descendants** outside of Japan. Japanese immigrants in the country, most from Okinawa, number 1.5 million people.

German immigrants have come in waves. There is a strong German influence particularly in the city of Blumenau in the South region of Brazil. The city has the second-largest Oktoberfest celebration in the world, with German folk dances, singing, and German food and drink.

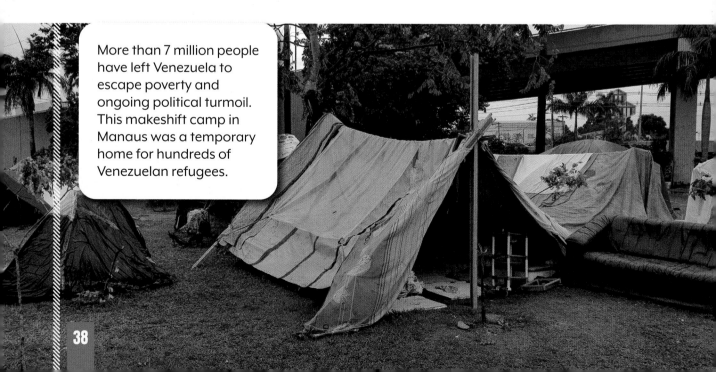

More than 7 million people have left Venezuela to escape poverty and ongoing political turmoil. This makeshift camp in Manaus was a temporary home for hundreds of Venezuelan refugees.

Timber-framed German architecture is common in Blumenau.

Millions of Italians immigrated to Brazil in the 1800s to work in mines and on plantations. They brought their culture with them, especially through their food. Catupiry cheese, used in many dishes including pizza, is a Brazilian cheese created by Italian immigrants.

Closer Look

Superstitions and Luck in Brazil

Many superstitions are rooted in religious belief. Others come from **folklore**. An itchy left hand is believed to be a sign that money is unexpectedly coming your way. It is considered bad luck, however, to leave a house through a different door than the one you entered. It is also bad luck to leave your handbag on the floor. Brazilians believe doing so will cause you to lose money. Each year, everyone wears white for New Year's Eve celebrations because they believe doing so will start the year with good luck and fortune.

Wearing white on New Year's Eve is believed to attract peace and symbolizes a fresh start for the new year.

Climate Change and Agriculture

Brazil has been one of the world's biggest emitters of greenhouse gases. These gases, such as carbon dioxide, trap heat close to Earth and raise its average temperatures. This rise in temperature, known as global warming, affects rain patterns, the strength of storms, and air and water temperatures.

A changing climate is resulting in challenges for the agriculture of Brazil. Ninety percent of Brazil's agriculture is rainfed. That means the water for crops and livestock comes from rain, rather than watering systems. This makes agriculture **vulnerable** to drought, heat waves, and other changes in weather patterns.

In June and July 2021, four rounds of severe frost greatly damaged the coffee crop in the state of Minas Gerais in Brazil. This has devastated coffee plantations, which need to be replanted.

Global warming is causing droughts to occur more often and for longer periods of time. With farmland drying up, livelihoods and food supplies are threatened. In 2022, thousands of farmers in southern Brazil were devastated by a drought that resulted in a loss of more than half of the overall soybean harvest.

To produce enough food during drought and flood conditions, more land is being cleared for agriculture. Large areas of the Amazon rain forest have been cut down to create more pasture for livestock. Deforestation in the Amazon is also due to illegal logging and mining. However, this makes the problem worse. Because trees store carbon dioxide, global warming speeds up when forests are cut down. Deforestation also causes more floods and droughts. Without trees to help soak in water, it runs away.

Under former president Jair Bolsonaro (2019–2022), average annual deforestation in the Amazon increased by 59.5 percent from the previous four years. Brazil's new government has enacted initiatives to stop the problem. The deforestation rate had already slowed by early 2023.

Closer Look

The average fully grown Amazon rainforest tree releases 264 gallons (1,000 liters) of water vapor into the atmosphere each day.

Flying Rivers

The Amazon rain forest creates huge amounts of **water vapor** as water evaporates off the trees' leaves, stems, and flowers. This water vapor rises into the air and is moved to other areas through wind and air currents, where it falls as rain. This process creates what are known as "flying rivers." Scientists say that without them, much of southern Brazil would be desert. As more of the rain forest is destroyed, however, flying rivers are smaller and fewer. Without the rainfall that comes from them, farmland in Brazil is drier, with fewer crops and livestock.

Brazilian farmers depend on the precipitation brought by the rain forest's flying rivers.

41

The Future of Mining

Bolsonaro wanted to grow the mining industry by opening up Indigenous lands to mining exploration. Bolsonaro has also been criticized for doing little to stop illegal mining in Brazil. In January 2023, Brazil declared a medical emergency in Yanomami Territory after it was reported that hundreds of Yanomami children had died from malnutrition and other diseases caused by mining pollution. The new Brazilian government has pledged to end mining on all Indigenous lands and impose restrictions on the supplies transported to illegal miners in the country.

A plan for sustainable mining has been underway with the help of government-funded studies. The plan's goal is to guide mining to expand and stay **profitable** until 2050. One strategy is to find investors and develop more mines for minerals needed for clean energy projects. The plan will also include regulations to protect the environment from the mining process.

In February 2021, the Amazonia 1 satellite was launched. It will be used to monitor deforestation, especially in the Amazon rain forest.

A Need for Sustainability

Brazil has made promises to reduce greenhouse gases that cause climate change. Ethanol fuel made from sugarcane can help reduce the use of fossil fuels such as gas and oil. Brazil has a new program called RenovaBio. Its goal is to help expand ethanol production. However, concerns with the program are that profits are too low to encourage more companies to use sugarcane for fuel. Initiatives for renewable energy are another way Brazil is tackling climate change.

COVID-19 Challenges

Industries in Brazil have been hit hard due to the COVID-19 pandemic. Brazil has had one of the highest death rates from the disease. This has disrupted employment, **supply chains**, and education. Education rates were already low in Brazil. Just 57 percent of adults in the country graduated high school. With pandemic school closures, the concern is that even more students are falling behind. A less-educated workforce means production is slower, unemployment is higher, and poverty increases.

A new solar farm is being built in Pirapora in the Southeast region of Brazil. The project will create more than 800 jobs and generate enough power for 1.4 million homes.

Tourism: Changes and Challenges

Tourism is a major part of Brazil's economy. Going forward, the tourism industry is facing challenges. World events and changing attitudes mean that this industry has to change too.

Because of the COVID-19 pandemic, the tourism industry in Brazil lost 94 billion dollars and more than 340,000 jobs from 2020 to 2022. The shutdowns and lockdowns in Brazil also resulted in loss of profits for businesses that rely on tourism. More than 50,000 businesses with links to tourism have closed for good, including 5,400 hotels. These closures may rebound with more people traveling, but tourism is changing. Many tourists are more interested in outdoor travel, away from cities and crowds. Visitors are heading to some of the lesser-known beaches along Brazil's long Atlantic coastline for quieter, less-crowded beach space. Tourists are also more interested in staying in holiday homes instead of large hotels.

President Bolsonaro received much criticism for his opposition to lockdowns, restrictions, and masking during the COVID-19 pandemic. Close to 700,000 deaths have been recorded in Brazil.

Ecotourism is on the rise, as is "bleisure" vacationing. This is a mix of "business" and "leisure." People are looking for vacation accommodations that allow them to do some work while away. As well as the usual facilities, accommodation for this kind of travel includes a work space and a fast Internet connection.

The new Environmental Crimes Law has been put in place to protect plant and animal species across Brazil. This is especially important in sensitive ecosystems such as the Amazon rain forest. The law sets restrictions on how the environment can be developed. It limits where and how many hotels can be built, how large they can be, and what other attractions, such as trails, zip lines, or tour routes, can be created. By protecting these ecosystems, Brazil can preserve the natural beauty and diversity of this amazing country.

The Pantanal wetland is a major site for ecotourism in Brazil. Tours use floating hotels or boat hotels to explore this ecosystem, home to jaguars, river otters, and anacondas.

amateur A person who does an activity for enjoyment

archaeological Related to human activity in history

biofuel Fuel made from living matter

carbon dioxide A greenhouse gas emitted when materials containing carbon are burned

cassava A root vegetable that grows in tropical climates

climate The usual, long-term weather conditions in a place

climate change A long-term change in the temperatures and weather patterns on Earth. Climate change often refers to global warming.

croquettes Small rolls of vegetables, meat, or fish fried in breadcrumbs

deforestation Clearing wide areas of forest

descendants People related to a particular ancestor from an earlier generation

double-cropping Growing two or more crops on the same piece of land in the same year

droughts Long periods with little or no rain

ecotourism Tourism focused on nature and conservation

empire A group of countries or colonies ruled by a single country or authority

enslaved People without rights or choice who are forced to work without pay

exporter A country, person, or company that sends goods to another country

extracting Removing

fast To restrict oneself from food or drink

fertile Land that is able to grow plants

floodplains Low-lying areas near rivers that flood when water levels are high

folklore The traditions, beliefs, and stories shared by a community

food security Having access to enough nutritious food all the time

freight Goods transported in large quantities by train, ship, plane, or truck

global warming The rise in Earth's temperature due to human activity

head One animal in a herd

hydroelectric Electricity generated by the power of moving water

Indigenous The first inhabitants of a place

industries Economic activities related to collecting and processing raw materials

inhabited Lived in

inland port A place where ships load or unload, away from the coast

instrumental Music performed with instruments but no voices

irrigation Supplying water to land so that plants and crops can grow

isolated Far away from other places and people

missionaries People sent to do religious work and spread their religion in another country

nomadic Moving from place to place

ore Rock that contains valuable minerals

originates Begins

pastureland Large areas where animals feed on grass

plantations Large farms on which crops are grown for profit

plateaus Large, mostly flat areas at higher elevations than the surrounding land

profitable Makes money

prospector Someone who explores an area for minerals and metals, such as gold

ravines Narrow valleys with steep sides

remote Located away from towns and villages

rice paddies Small flooded fields where rice is grown

samba A Brazilian dance that originated in Africa

sediment Small pieces of material that sink to the bottom of water or liquid

self-sufficient Not needing outside help

semi-arid A dry area, but with a little more rain than a desert

shamans Priests or priestesses who use plants, herbs, and magic for curing the sick

slave trade The capturing, buying, and selling of enslaved people

Southern Hemisphere The half of Earth that is south of the equator

supply chains Networks of companies and people in the production and delivery of items

textile Cloth or woven fabric

torrential Very heavy; falling rapidly

toxic Poisonous

tributaries Rivers or streams that flow into a larger river or lake

uncontacted Isolated from other cultures and people

undergrowth Plants growing under trees in a forest

UNESCO World Heritage Site A protected landmark or area singled out by the United Nations Educational, Scientific, and Cultural Organization (UNESCO) as being globally significant

unpopulated Not occupied or settled by people

volume The amount of space that a substance takes up, such as the amount of water in a river

vulnerable More easily attacked or damaged

water vapor Water that has changed to gas

World War II The 1939–1945 war between the Axis powers (Germany, Japan, and Italy) and the Allies (mainly the UK and its colonies, the U.S., and the Soviet Union)

Books

Aloian, Molly. *The Amazon: River in a Rain Forest*. Crabtree Publishing, 2010.

Hyde, Natalie. *Amazon Rainforest Research Journal*. Crabtree Publishing, 2018.

Sexton, Colleen. *Brazil*. Bellwether Media, 2010.

Websites

https://kids.nationalgeographic.com/geography/countries/article/brazil
Learn all about Brazil's physical geography, history, wildlife, people, and culture with National Geographic Kids.

https://www.pbs.org/journeyintoamazonia/about.html
Take a "Journey into Amazonia" and learn all about the unique species and natural wonders of the Amazon rain forest.

https://wwf.panda.org/discover/knowledge_hub/where_we_work/amazon/about_the_amazon/people_amazon/
Learn more about the Indigenous peoples of the Amazon rain forest.

https://rioandlearn.com/dances-from-brazil/
Read about and watch videos showing different kinds of vibrant Brazilian dances. Then, explore other pages on Brazilian instruments, music, and musicians.

About the Author

Natalie Hyde has written over 100 fiction and non-fiction books for young readers. Exploring new cultures, traditions, and of course, food, is something she loves to do on her travels.